Wilderness Survival Skills:

Learn How To Survive in The Wild if You Have Just a Knife

Table of Contents

Introduction

We have at least a passing fascination with survival. Well it becomes much more of a big deal when it is a must. If you do not have any skills in bushcraft, you'r screwed. Disaster strikes, you better hope you get rescued. Otherwise, you'll want to read on.

Bushcraft involves the skills needed to survive in the wilderness or the "bush". It is not about having a bunch of equipment. It's much more about what you lack than what you have. While there are many programs on television and films depicting bushcraft, these are not skills that most feel important to have. It is typically only in terms of some version of disaster or end of the world scenario that people realize how important these basic survival skills are.

There are those who were in girl or boy scouts or some other wilderness group as a youth, however, not many others have any true bushcraft skills. People today are so dependent on technology that the answer that occurs to them is either to Google it or there is an app for that.

Without the option of smartphones and internet, most would dissolve into complete panic and lose all sense of themselves. It is essential to recognize that cell towers can fail, wi-fi can suddenly stop, as well as most other modern conveniences. Nature is the ultimate and while humans have spent the bulk of our existence distancing ourselves from nature, people must teach themselves and their children skills for basic survival.

Unfortunately, it is usually not until bushcraft is needed that people realize they have no intelligence at all in the area. At one point camping was a regular thing for people growing up which they maintained for their children, but people no longer seek to become one with nature, not usually until nature comes to them. There are many scenarios, some extreme, some not so extreme, when bushcraft can save your life. It could be as big as plane crash survival or as small as your car stopping during a road trip in the middle of nowhere.

It could be that a major storm knocks out all electrical power and you are cut off or your kid wants an outdoor adventure. Whether you are doing it for sport or because you really must keep yourself alive, it is always better to know bushcraft and not need it than to need it and not know it. There are many different elements required to be a master at bushcraft and once you are you will feel like a cowboy or original human being.

From making fire to hunting, foraging, building shelter, tying knots, woodworking, tracking, and making use of a knife, there are few things more satisfying than mastering those skills that first made man sustainable against nature. Ask yourself, what would you do in the wilderness armed with nothing but a knife? If you have no idea, this book is for you.

Chapter 1 – Getting Crafty In The Bush

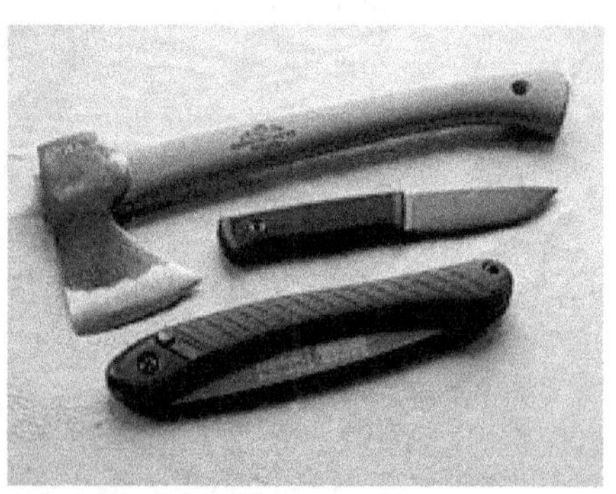

Some of you may have read books like Lord of the Flies, Robinson Crusoe, or Walden and think you have a pretty good idea of what bushcraft is. Really though, most haven't the foggiest idea of what it would take to survive with their only real tool being a knife. One of the most basic things of importance is to be sure that the knife that one has is enough to get them through.

Obviously a basic butter knife will not fulfill your needs. You will need something far more advanced, such as a hunter's knife. The knife should be relatively short, sharp, yet lightweight. The ideal size for a bushcraft knife is between 3 - 5 inches long, 3 - 5 mm thick, and 5-7 ounces. Long knifes are subject to break, particularly with everything that you will need to do with it.

Swiss army knives are good for its many different compartments, yet the actual blade itself is usually lacking. If one is building a survival kit, it is best to stock it with a slender, durable blade, as well as a small axe and shorter blade to be used for cooking.

If one is lucky enough or smart enough to have built a kit before hand there are some important things to include. You will want to pack as light as possible, so that means including items which can be used for a multitude of purposes. Tin foil is great, light weight, and thin, yet incredibly useful. It is malleable enough to be able to fit around practically anything.

It can be formed to be bowl or cup-like to drink or eat from. It can be placed over your water to make it boil faster. It will decrease the cooking time on anything. Another very useful tool for the kit are garbage bags. They are thin and very portable. They can be used to pack leaves up and used as bedding material. Duct tape is great for binding or patching up. Sandwich bag and straw can be used for water.

Things such as wire, string, coal, a compass, small knife sharpener, lighter, flares, hand mirrors, small first aid kit, collapsible cups or pots, and canteen or flask are all great for a kit. These items do not take up much space and are easy to carry around. Obviously you can't pack up your TV or your fridge, so you'll have to use the most simple items to achieve your survival needs.

That is if you get to put together a kit. If not and your knife is all you have, all is not lost. Bushcraft is about what is at your disposal. You cannot harp on what you don't have. You must be creative enough to compensate for what is lacking. Should disaster strike, whatever the cause, you must be able to proceed or you are toast.

The most important thing would be to steady yourself and begin to prioritize. The first thing is to get a running mental list of what you will need to survive. Our basic human needs are food, water, and shelter.

In any area you might find yourself, there will be any number of people or animals around which you cannot be sure are dangerous or harmless. The best thing to equip yourself with in life is a good range of knowledge. Bushcraft is about recognition of what is around you. If you can't tell a Birch tree from a Pine tree, you're going to be in trouble.

You must be able to identify the best solutions in nature. Take the time to study tree classifications and uses. Know some fungi species. Knowledge is about the best weapon one can have. Your first instinct will be to panic, but when you have a basic understanding of what nature provides, there is no need to panic.

If you're on a camping trip or a leisurely tryst into nature you'll be able to enjoy it's peacefulness quite easily. If you are dealing with life or death you'll be in a much more frantic state. If The Walking Dead has taught you nothing else, don't get ahead of yourself.

Our scenario is one in which only real tool at your disposal is a knife. A knife is a lot more useful than most would think. It is important to know the many uses into which a knife can be put. Here are some tips to maximize knife usage.

1. Careful using your knife, because if you stick yourself you're putting yourself in a position to have to provide medical care which will only worsen your situation. Your mother taught you not to run with scissors. Do not be too reckless with your knife.

2. You can use bramble or other thin stems from plants to tie your knife to the end of a branch at whick point it can be used as a kind of spear.

3. Another great tip in using your knife is to use it in conjunction with a nice sized branch, both long and respectably thick. You can use the branch to bang your knife through thicker trees and wood.

4. Anything smaller you may need to burn either to melt or reshape you can poke your knife through and use to put it in the fire safely. If you have a shot gun shell you can use the knife to shape it into an arrowhead.

5. Whittling will be a major facet of your survival. Obviously the outside bark on trees and branches will be more rough and dirty. Cutting through it with chopping motions with your knife gets through to smoother wood, sap, and anything else needed within the tree.

6. The knife can be used to help in climbing as well. With your branch you can bang it into wood or rock and create spaces for foot and hand placement.

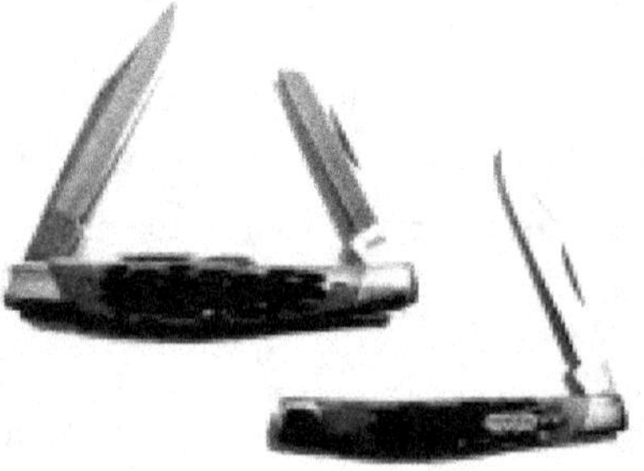

7. Knives can be used to start fire. If you have another piece of metal, striking it hard in a downward swipe with your knife is an easy way to produce a spark to get your fire going.

8. It is a weapon. The most basic weapon aside from your body. Knife skills in combat or to ward off attack is crucial. Hold your knife with the blade just beyond your fingertips while gripping the butt with your palm for added power. Also holding it away from your body at a perpendicular angle when under attack can offer more dangerous strikes while keeping you at lesser risks.

9. The blade is not the only useful part of the knife. The butt can also be used as a hammering mechanism. Be sure to cover the blade when using it this way as not to cut yourself.

10. There will be digging involved. A knife is not the ideal shovel, but it can be very effective. Whether your digging holes to build a strong foundation or digging for materials, your knife is your friend. Again, proper holding techniques go a long

way, not only in safety, but also in effectiveness. The way you hold a knife can be important depending on the impact you care trying to make.

With nothing more than a knife by your side, that knife must become your everything. It can't be your phone and it doesn't come with wi-fi, but it is still pretty cool. It will be a necessary tool at all levels of survival. It will be your weapon, enable the creation of all that is required to maintain on your own, and be all you need to do anything.

We are so fortunate, we take so much for granted. We have so many conveniences at our daily disposal. Without them we feel lost. It will take a great deal of imagination and intelligence to discern how to make use of what you have. You must remember that there was a time in history when people did not even have a knife and yet they found a way to survive. It is one of the first human technologies along with fire and the wheel. Treat it with the reverence it deserves and recognize that in bushcraft a knife is as vital as anything you could have outside of a society set up with all the conveniences you could desire.

Be sure with your knife and know that in whatever situation you may find yourself, that knife can be a key part of the solution. Whatever you need to do your hands and your knife can do. With all of the things we use in our day to day lives it is hard to believe that such basic tools could be all we need. However, through bushcraft we can come to understand that we live in excess and really we do not need all of the luxuries that we think we do. We can in fact live with a knife and a plan. One of the first things on the docket must be shelter.

Chapter 2 – The Sleeps

Even being out in the wilderness we need at least some sense of shelter. It is possible that you could find a cave or some kind of enclosure, but it is not likely. Even if you do it is not likely that it is not occupied or in danger of some animal or other person coming in. It may not seem so, but it is far more secure to find an unoccupied area that does not have any evidence of tracks or creatures and set up your lodgings there.

Worst case scenario you will not have a proper tent, so you will need to use your knife to make one. That means you will have to search the area for anything that can be used to close in a space away from bugs and other outdoor nuisances. Cutting down trees and bushes will work, though it may take some time to get enough for coverage. It is a lot more thorough to try and build something more like a cabin. If you have a small axe, you can hack at surrounding trees and wood to pull together a nice, makeshift house. It does not have to be perfect, just secure from weather and animals.

Here are some hacks on how to live relatively comfortably in the wild:

1. You'll want to gather as much material as possible. Leaves, tree bark, feathers, durable branches and stems are all materials that will build a nice home for you. Keep your eyes open for anything you can find that can be put to good use.

2. If you have a kit and it has trash bags in it, you have what you need for a bed. Feel the bags with dried leaves and feathers which can provide a decent mattress of sorts and pillows.

3. If you do not have a kit with materials, that's alright. You can construct a raised bed starting with the trunks of young trees and stack it with thinner branches which can be tied together.

4. Look for as much grass and leaves as possible to try and achieve some comfort. Pine sap can be melted down to provide adhesive to keep things together. A lot of tree sap can have a similar function. If you are lucky enough to be near living, well watered plants you will be able to get softer leaves and flowers. Moss can also work

well, though almost certain to be damp. Otherwise you'll have to make the best of what you have.

5. Leaves and grass is not just for coverage, but also for insulation. Stuff your makeshift bed and clothes with the dried leaves to provide extra warmth in cooler climates.

6. Hack away at tree bark, which will be the best material you can find. Birch tree bark in particular is sturdy. It can act as a roof to shield you from inclimate weather. Obviously the bigger the trees the better.

7. Look for pine, spruce, and fir trees in particular. They provide the best insulation. Birch is good as well. Use fallen trees as a shelf.

8. In order to make branches more durable, cut off the bark and hold over fire. You want to hold it close enough to heat, but not too close or it will catch fire. You will be able to see the transformation over time.

9. Use your knife to whittle thicker branches into wedges. They will make it easier both to pound through to break up wood and to make things sturdier.

10. In the movies you see people collecting really thick tree trunks for things. You do not need to do that. Branches and smaller trunks are fine, easier to get to, and require less strength. Though you are preparing to rest, no need to over-exert yourself.

For those masters in bushcraft, they will be able to take their knife and between wood, leaves, and animal skin tie together a respectable shelter. It's all about being able to get yourself and everything that you make or acquire into something that is completely yours. It is always better to put as much between you and the elements as you can.

Your first suit of armor is your clothing. Again, it is about compensation. You must be able to make up for what you don't already have. Be sure to stretch the branches to insure they are durable. Stick durable branches as deep in the ground as you can to create a sound base. You may also want to litter your area with twigs and crunchier grass so that you can hear anything entering your camp.

It is also important to know the difference in what lives where and what is poisonous. You will need to be able to have a general distinction between bugs and other smaller creatures. You don't want to go surrounding yourself with ants or poisonous spiders because you're cutting up trees full of them.

Pay attention and try not to rush. You are in a very urgent situation, but as much as is possible, maintain a cool head and keep yourself grounded. Keep telling yourself you have everything you need to survive. Now, this is the case in the worst case scenario where you have to find the means of survival.

If you are choosing to put yourself into the wild or the bush then the mind frame is different, but the technique is the same. Keep your mind on your work, don't rush it, and everything will work out for the best.

If at all possible, try to train yourself and your children in normal circumstances so that when your survival instincts do kick in it is coming from prior knowledge. You can learn on your feet, but it's always better to be prepared.

Be conscious of a few safety tips: First of all, do not set up a fire too close by. Like Smokey the Bear used to say, "You too can prevent forest fires." Don't build yourself up a beautiful camp just to burn it down. That may seem like common sense to some, but not so much to others.

The best way is to create a sort of barrier between the fire and your sleeping space. It is better to try and situate yourself off of the ground, perhaps creating a sort of hammock and covering it up in as much material as you can find. Not to make it heavy, but to make it solid. Bear in mind that this shelter is temporary and that even in the best scenario will only last for a few days.

It is better to keep moving as opposed to wait for something to come along and force you to leave. Hope that weather will be kind to you, but do not count on it. As the saying goes, hope for the best, but prepare for the worst.

Use some of your tree bark to construct boxes. It is always better to have storage as opposed to having to expend energy on going out each time you need something. Also be cautious because even the best made tent or cabin will only shield you for so long.

That is why you keep your knife on your body at all times. Do not put it down for any reason. You must be able to grab for it at a moment's notice. Make some kind of sheath to keep it safely on you, either out of thick leaves or a small patch of your own clothing.

You do not want to risk being disoriented and having to look for your knife at the same time. Your knife needs to become your best friend. If need be, you may want to try and make another. Ther is a chance that you could find some metal or simply just sharpen a knife.

One way or another, the more you have the better. You need not only to make yourself shelter, but be able and prepared to defend it. Life in the wild is no joke and it is important not to get too comfortable. Be alert. Sleep is a necessity and will allow for the energy to be able get the other necessities: food and water.

Chapter 3 – The Eats

You will need to eat and there may be McDonalds in a lot of places, but they are nowhere in the bush. You will have to find food for yourself. The first key is to be able to identify what is safe to eat and what is not. Here are some tips for feeding in the woods:

1. First of all, grass is always safe to eat. It may not taste great and there may be some sanitary concerns, but you can eat it. It's simple, it's easy, it's right there.

2. There are plenty of natural teas that can be made in the wild. Dandelion tea is good, good for you, and has health benefits. Acorns can also be boiled and used for a medicinal tea.

3. If you do not have that much food, eat at night, that is when you will most need it. Your body will be trying to conduct heat, so it needs food as fuel.

4. Chewing on dark leaf sap will give you natural antihistamines in case you touch poison or something of that nature. Chew the leaves.

5. Chewing on willow tree bark will help with most pains, particularly cold and fever.

6. In humid areas the food is in the sun. Elsewhere it is near the water. Fruiting trees in particular are found near water.

7. Berries on ornamental shrubs are edible.

8. You can eat cattail, bulrush, watercress, daylilies, honeysuckle, violets, rose, greenbriar, and deciduous leaves from linden, sassafras, and sourwood. Do not, I repeat, DO NOT eat azaleas.

9. Clovers are lucky for a reason. You can eat them. There is also such a thing as wild asparagus.

10. Here are some of the clear markers of things you should not eat: Sap that is milky or discolored, spines, fine hairs, thorns, pods that have beans, bulbs, or seeds inside, if it tastes bitter or soapy, dill, carrot, parsnip, or parsley-shaped foliage, woody parts and leaves with an almond scent, pink, purplish, or black spurs on grain heads, and patterns of three-leaved growth.

Remember that the food is to nourish you, not to kill you, so be aware of what is safe to eat and what is not. It would be wonderful if there was just a farm to go to and get all the food you desire, but that is not realistic to a survival situation. Foraging and hunting will more than likely be your only means of nourishment.

Obviously, if you are of a smaller build you will want to go for smaller animals. Squirrels, birds, rabbits, that sort of thing. In your kit, pack rat traps. Much more effective than you would think. Understand that you are not the only predator out there and you may have to compete with other animals for that prey. You can try to get them with your bare hands, or you can construct traps for the animals to get caught in. Lure them with food.

Do not try and catch anything you are not prepared to kill. Bigger animals will last longer, but that will also mean a fight. If you are not prepared to wrestle with a deer, you may want to keep it small. Try and stock up as much as possible so that you do not spend all of your time hunting.

You can get water to drink and clean yourself with, as well as fish. It may seem that sticking your hand in the water and pulling out a fish is perfectly plausible, but that will require a level of skill that you most likely do not possess. It is far easier and more logical to make yourself a fishing mechanism.

Cut a good, sturdy branch, no more than 5 or 6 inches, tie it with string or branches in the middle and tie the end with bait. Lower it into the water and when you feel the fish grabbing, start reeling it in by rolling the small long forward which will wrap up the string.

Presto, chango, you've got yourself a fish. Keep your eyes peeled for other predators who eat fish. Depending on where you are you may be competing with anywhere from seagulls to bears to alligators. Have some awareness of where you are and what you are up against.

Try and use the fur from the animals as either clothing or shelter. The food will need to be cooked and be aware of the animal appears to be diseased in any way. For fish, you will need to remove the scales and get down to the meat inside. Whatever water you get for yourself will not be sanitary.

Make sure to sterilize before trying to drink it. Create a natural filter using grass, sand, and charcoal stacked together. These will get out grit of all kinds. You may also use a clean cloth to pour through. Boil the water over your fire to ensure that it is safe for consumption.

That is a crucial step that cannot be missed. You have no idea what has been in that water. Do not drink until it has been boiled. If you have your tin foil, place that over your container to speed up the process. You can make a simple pot hook using one forked branch, one hooked branch and a straight one to go across. Put your hooked and forked branches in the ground and the other across on top.

The pot or kettle will give it the balance to secure it. If you are not near a river or stream, moss can be wrung out to get water. It won't taste the best, but it gets the job done. As does the dew on the grass first thing in the morning.

Do not over-eat. As humans we are used to over-consuming, but when trying to survive that can definitely go against you. You need the energy, but over-eating can slow you down and make you susceptible should you find yourself in a dire situation. Stay as light as possible. Once you are no longer hungry, store the remainder of your food.

Use your constructed containers and put the food up where it can not be taken. It is most secure to keep the food with you, but that will mean maintaining a relatively small store. Also try not to be too fragrant or you are guaranteed to attract other predators. It is all about being smart and safe. Things in nature tend to know how much is necessary for survival.

What humans are supposed to have on animals is the ability to form more complex ideas. So be wise in foraging and hunting. Do not bite off more than you can chew, literally or figuratively. Use your knife to your advantage and do not try to accomplish fantastic feats just to get food. Getting energy is important, but so is conservation of energy.

One of the keys to bushcraft is simplicity. Do not overdo anything and do not be greedy. We are taught our whole lives as humans that we are superior, but know that our many technologies and luxuries have crippled us in real ways and so when faced with the wilderness we can be at a disadvantage. In recapturing our primal instinct, know that we can be our own worst enemies. So eat when you must, eat light, and do not attempt anything too big for your knife or your fire.

Chapter 4 – Let There Be Fire

Fire is one of the original human creations that set us apart and above nature. Fire can occur naturally, but that is wild fire. We can learn to create and tame it at will and that is one of the most important facets of bushcraft. Honestly, without the ability to make a fire, your knife nor anything else can do you any good. You will freeze and/or starve to death if you cannot make a fire. But again, be aware that fire can be the best and worst thing you do.

Be conscious of how and where you conjure your fire and be sure that it does not roar out of control. If you are too reckless with it it will consume you and everything around you. Fire is a beautiful, wonderful thing when handled correctly. It can also be your worst nightmare. You can wield it as a weapon, but be advised that it can be a danger to you and whatever you are trying to use it against. Here are some useful tips on how to make and maintain a fire:

1. We often see firewood as logs. It is more practical and advisable to use twigs.

2. Clear the ground where you are building the fire to keep it from spreading. Make a little pit for it.

3. Coal fungus, marked by it's resemblance to charcoal, is great for kindling. It is usually attached to dead fallen trees.

4. Other great tinder for fire is bark from birch trees, feathers, dead pine needles, and pine cones.

5. Again, if you have a piece of metal with your knife you can strike a fire very easily.

6. If not, cut two thick branches, thin one out with your knife, cut the bark off of the other one, but keep it round. Place the thin one on the ground and put the rounded one about two inches in from the tip. Using string, or your shoelaces, wrap the smooth rounded branch about four time and grip it tightly. Placing your foot to keep the flat branch on the ground, quickly pull the rounded branch back and forth, creating a fast, spinning motion. Keep grinding it down until you see smoke. Voila, fire!

7. Take some kindling and get it smoking with embers. It will start small, so to cause it to spread quickly without going out, you will need to pick it up and gently blow on it until it is a small fire. Make sure you have enough kindling so that you don't burn your hands.

8. If it has been raining, simply cut the bark off of the branches to get to the dry inside.

9. Gather large branches full of pine to place over your fire and to create a smoke signal when in distress.

10. To use your fire to keep your shoes and clothes dry, create a simple rack. On both sides of the fire drive in two sticks each, forked, and then place two long sticks across the top. Make it long enough so that the things don't burn.

Fire can be used for a few different things. It can be used to sterilize things, particularly in situations where injuries arise. Whatever medical attention you try to give yourself or others, make sure to sterilize your knife with fire. It is mostly used for cooking, sterilizing water, and though warmth.

You can carry fire around, either by confining it to a jar or carrying it around on something that is flammable, yet will not be over-consumed with the flames. Controlling a fire is as important as making it. It is of little use to you to set the entire place on fire. It must be big enough, yet small enough at the same time. For extra precaution, build a fort around it out of sticks to keep it inside of it. Fire is just one of the many tools that will aid in survival in the bush. Mastering it is a major skill, but not the only.

Chapter 5 – Emphasis On The Craft

We have gone through the most basic things needed to survive. Once you have your shelter, food, and fire down, you will realize that there is even more required in survival. There will be instances of injury, travel, combat, and other things that come up and need tools. Your knife is a great base and can serve you in many things, but it will take more.

Having a keen mind for sustainable and necessary materials will be a real life saver. You must keep your eyes open and recognize what will be of good use to you. The issue will be the necessity to travel light, so it will be a constant game of determining what is important and what is not. Here are some extra tips that will help you thrive in the bush:

1. Rubbing raw crab apples in a womb will help to heal it.

2. Smear charcoal under eyes to reduce glare from sun. That is why football players do it.

3. You may also cut eye slits into tree bark and tie it over your face like a mask.

4. Grind charcoal & add some water to create toothpaste. It can get the teeth clean without damaging them.

5. Boiling down sap and syrup from trees will leave a sticky residue that can be used as glue.

6. Look for vines, thin, tough branches, and tough stems for tying materials.

7. You can make a stove by cutting a log in four, tying the pieces together in a circle with a few inches of space between them, placing a short log inside, putting kindling on top of the short log, and lighting it. Make sure the log pieces are higher than the kindling.

8. If you do have a kit or backpack, hang it from a tree, but instead of using the branches on the tree already, which can be flimsy, place your own entwined branches in the fork of the tree.

9. The small hand mirror can be used to signal for help. Angle it to catch the sunlight.

10. If you do not have a compass, look up at the sun at noon which will be North. 2pm in the winter.

It all seems like fun and games, but that is because we take so much for granted. We buy things as opposed to having to make every little thing for ourselves. It will be hard, but very possible. Even if initially you are only armed with a knife. That knife can be the genesis for all else that is required to survive. Take wood shop or any other training that weans you off of the many luxuries that you enjoy on the daily. Whether you want to give up typical societal living for that of Walden or just take the time to expand behind civilization, bushcraft is a essential set of skills that can truly show what humanity is capable of.

Conclusion

I hope now you have a better appreciation for bushcraft and the possibilities of life with just you and a knife. It seems crazy to think of, but we are all too capable of sustaining ourself no matter the situation or its cause.

We have seen time and time again that people even in the worst scenarios can and will thrive in the face of nature and its strength. We have all thought about the deserted island scenario, but it does not have to be as far fetched as that.

We can never know what will come and snatch everything away. With global warming kicking up more and more we are constantly being reminded how fickle everything is. It may not be a zombie apocalypse, but there can be a major event that makes all we have useless.

We must prepare ourselves to survive in the most base environment or else we are doomed. Bushcraft may seem like skills fit for cavemen, but they can be far more handy than one may imagine. Life may seem easy depending on others, but that may just be an illusion.

So tomorrow terror strikes, all hell breaks lose, and civilization completely crumbles. But that's okay, because you have read this book and now at least have a basic understanding of what it will take to survive. Use this as a starting off point and get yourself out there and sharpen your skills.

Realize that bushcraft, either in its simplest form or its most advanced, is not only a cool set of skills to have in the arsenal, but should be basic learning for all. Teach yourself bushcraft now while you are choosing too and you will find yourself in scenarios where you will be grateful you did in the future.

If you have not grabbed it yet, please go ahead and download your special bonus report *"Preppers Survival Guide. Proven Tactics For Armed Incounters!"*

Simply Click the Button Below

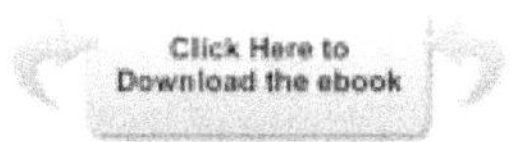

OR **Go to This Page**

http://preppersliving.com/free

BONUS #2: More Free & Discounted Books & Products

Do you want to receive more Free/Discounted Books or Products?

We have a mailing list where we send out our new Books or Products when they go free or with a discount on Amazon. Click on the link below to sign up for Free & Discount Book & Product Promotions.

=> Sign Up for Free & Discount Book & Product Promotions <=

OR Go to this URL

http://zbit.ly/1WBb1Ek